S0-EGR-721

THE WILD WEST TRIVIA SERIES:

LEWIS & CLARK

TRIVIA

BY RICK STEBER

ISBN: 978-0-945134-49-7

Printed and bound in the United States of America by
Maverick Publications • Bend, Oregon

THE WILD WEST TRIVIA SERIES:

Lewis and Clark Trivia is one book from the Wild West Trivia series. Each book is designed to challenge a reader's knowledge and expertise relating to American history, the great outdoors and the wide panorama of the Western landscape. This series is educational and a fun way for children, friends and families to learn. Oftentimes a question or answer will serve as a springboard into other discussions, remembrances or related stories.

Turn *Lewis and Clark Trivia* into an entertaining game by having one person read a question aloud. The opponent, or team of players, selects an answer.

The reader turns the page and reads aloud the correct answer. This is a wonderful way to pass the miles while traveling, or as rousing entertainment around a crackling campfire. Have fun while you learn, and keep score if you wish. Collect the entire series.

QUESTION

In what year did President Thomas Jefferson propose an expedition be sent to explore the interior and far western reaches of the North American continent?

    A. 1776
    B. 1803
    C. 1811

ANSWER ON
NEXT PAGE

1

ANSWER

B

On January 18, 1803, in a secret message to Congress, President Thomas Jefferson proposed an expedition be sent to explore the interior and far west. This became the Corps of Volunteers for Northwestern Discovery, shortened to the Corps of Discovery and finally to the Corps.

QUESTION

How many men were permanent members of the Lewis and Clark Expedition?

    A. 12
    B. 33
    C. 64

ANSWER ON
NEXT PAGE

3

ANSWER

The Lewis and Clark Expedition departed Fort Wood with 33 permanent members, including soldiers, hunters, blacksmiths, gunsmiths, boatmen, carpenters, cooks, woodsmen and interpreters. At the Mandan Indian village on the Missouri River, Toussaint Charbonneau, his wife Sacagawea and their baby Pomp joined the permanent crew.

4

QUESTION

Why was it decided that two men should share command of the Corps of Discovery?

- A. Better control of the men
- B. More efficient line of command
- C. Someone else to take the blame if the expedition failed

ANSWER ON NEXT PAGE

ANSWER

President Jefferson and Meriwether Lewis decided a co-commander would allow a more efficient line of command in the event Lewis became seriously ill or even died. William Clark, Lewis's commanding officer in the army, was chosen as co-commander. Clark had wilderness experience and was an excellent map maker.

QUESTION

Which member of the Corps of Discovery worked as private secretary to President Jefferson?

- A. Meriwether Lewis
- B. William Clark
- C. George Drouillard

ANSWER ON
NEXT PAGE

ANSWER

Meriwether Lewis served as private secretary to President Jefferson. In 1809, enroute to Washington, D.C., he died of gunshot wounds at an inn in Tennessee. Some scholars believe Lewis suffered from mental depression and committed suicide, others are of the opinion he was murdered by highwaymen.

QUESTION

Which President of the United States was Thomas Jefferson?

    A. Third
    B. Fifth
    C. Seventh

ANSWER ON
NEXT PAGE

ANSWER

Thomas Jefferson, one of the founders of the United States and author of the Declaration of Independence, became the third President of the United States and served two terms, from 1800 to 1808. He maintained a lifelong fascination with the West.

QUESTION

Along the lower Missouri River, members of the Corps killed a pelican. How many gallons of water were they able to pour in the pelican's pouch?

    A. Two gallons
    B. Three gallons
    C. Five gallons

ANSWER ON
NEXT PAGE

ANSWER

As the men traversed the lower Missouri they encountered a three-mile long blanket of white feathers covering the river. The source was a pelican rookery on an island. Captain Lewis ordered a specimen be taken and while conducting an examination of the bird it was discovered that the pelican's expandable beak pouch held five gallons of water.

QUESTION

When William Clark climbed Hill of the Little Devils what did he see?

A. Indians
B. Elk and buffalo
C. Little devils

ANSWER ON
NEXT PAGE

13

ANSWER

B

As the Expedition traveled up the Missouri River little could be seen of the surrounding countryside until they reached a mound the Indians feared, believing tiny humanlike devils lived there. Clark climbed to the top of the mound, which he named Hill of the Little Devils, and wrote in his journal that he counted more than 800 elk and buffalo grazing nearby.

14

QUESTION

Name the animal that Captain Lewis called barking squirrel.

    A. Coyote
    B. Fox
    C. Prairie dog

ANSWER ON
NEXT PAGE

ANSWER

On September 7, 1804, Lewis and Clark found themselves in a landscape of earthen mounds inhabited by small animals that, when alarmed, whistled loudly and plunged into their burrows. Lewis called these animals "barking squirrels", Clark called them "ground rats", but Sergeant John Ordway, who called them "prairie dogs", proposed the name that stuck.

16

QUESTION

Name the event that occurred in 1792 which helped to establish American claim to the Northwest Territory?

- A. Discovery of the Northwest Passage
- B. Louisiana Purchase
- C. Captain Gray discovers the mouth of the Columbia River

ANSWER ON NEXT PAGE

17

ANSWER

Captain Robert Gray, an American, sailed into the Columbia River in 1792 and laid claim to all the land drained by this mighty river in the name of the United States.

QUESTION

The Louisiana Purchase included all land in the watershed of which great North American river?

    A. Missouri River
    B. Mississippi River
    C. Columbia River

ANSWER ON
NEXT PAGE

19

ANSWER

The exact boundaries of the land acquired by the United States in the Louisiana Purchase was open to debate. However, it was generally accepted that the territory purchased included all the land in the Missouri River drainage.

QUESTION

When the United States opened negotiations with France which would eventually lead to the Louisiana Purchase, what was the United States hoping to acquire?

A. All land drained by the Mississippi River
B. Seaport on the Gulf of Mexico
C. Western half of the North American continent

ANSWER ON NEXT PAGE

ANSWER

The Louisiana Purchase originated from an attempt by the United States to purchase the seaport of New Orleans. It was the belief of government officials that to have access to the Gulf of Mexico and to control the mouth of the Mississippi River was in the best interests of the United States.

QUESTION

The Missouri River is most famous as?

    A. Longest river in the United States
    B. Widest river in the United States
    C. River with the largest flow of water
       in the United States

ANSWER ON
NEXT PAGE

ANSWER

The Missouri River is the longest river in the United States. It flows 2,466 miles and is the chief tributary of the Mississippi River. Together these two great rivers form the nation's major waterway.

QUESTION

In what current state are the headwaters of the Missouri River?

    A. Oregon
    B. Montana
    C. North Dakota

ANSWER ON
NEXT PAGE

25

ANSWER

The Missouri River is formed in southeastern Montana by the Jefferson, Madison and Gallatin rivers. Descending from the Rocky Mountains these combined rivers flow north, then east, across Montana.

QUESTION

Where does the Missouri River join the
Mississippi River?

    A. It never joins the Mississippi River
    B. North of St. Louis
    C. North of New Orleans

ANSWER ON
NEXT PAGE

ANSWER

B

The Missouri River joins the Mississippi River north of St. Louis, making the combined river the largest in the United States. The Lewis and Clark Expedition set up their winter camp here, on the east side of the Mississippi River directly across from the mouth of the Missouri River. They called this place Camp Wood and also referred to it as Camp Dubois.

QUESTION

What did President Jefferson direct Lewis and Clark to search for?

- A. Mastodons
- B. Gold
- C. Strategic military post locations

ANSWER ON
NEXT PAGE

29

ANSWER

President Jefferson's directives to the Expedition included a number of goals: to find a practical waterway across the continent, record information about plant and animal life, map geographical features, establish peaceful relations with the Indians, and to search for Ice Age creatures, including mastodons, which were thought to still roam the Plains and the Far West.

QUESTION

What did the men of the Corps use to write in their journals?

- A. Pencils
- B. Ball-point pens
- C. Quill pens and ink

ANSWER ON
NEXT PAGE

31

ANSWER

The men wrote in their journals at night by candlelight or campfire light, using quill pens and ink. When the weather was bad they would write very little and try to catch up when conditions were more favorable.

QUESTION

Meriwether Lewis directed William Clark to find men to employee for the Expedition who possessed what particular quality?

    A. Intelligence
    B. Intimate knowledge of the West
    C. Unmarried

ANSWER ON
NEXT PAGE

ANSWER

Lewis established several criteria for the men employed for the Expedition. First and foremost they were to be single men with no attachments to draw them away from a two-year commitment. In addition Lewis wrote, they were to be "good hunters, stout, healthy, accustomed to the woods, and capable of bearing bodily fatigue in a pretty considerable degree."

QUESTION

What musical instrument was brought by two members of the Lewis and Clark Expedition?

- A. Harmonica
- B. Guitar
- C. Fiddle

ANSWER ON
NEXT PAGE

ANSWER

Two men, Pierre Cruzatte and George Gibson, brought their fiddles. They played them around the campfire to entertain the members of the Expedition as well as the Indians they encountered along the way.

QUESTION

Who was the only African-American member of the Lewis and Clark Expedition?

    A. York
    B. Boston
    C. Jim Jackson

ANSWER ON
NEXT PAGE

ANSWER

York was William Clark's slave and the first man with black skin many Indians had seen. York's presence was especially beneficial when meeting the Arikara, Mandan, Shoshone and Nez Perce Indians. Upon his return to civilization, York was granted his freedom by Clark. He is thought to have died of cholera, about 1832, while on his way to visit Clark.

QUESTION

As the Lewis and Clark Expedition started up the Missouri River, who was the youngest member of the party?

- A. Patrick Gass
- B. Charles Floyd
- C. George Shannon

ANSWER ON
NEXT PAGE

39

ANSWER

George Shannon was only 18 years old when he joined the Lewis and Clark Expedition. After returning from the Expedition Shannon was severely wounded in an Indian attack and his leg was amputated. He became an attorney and later served as a Senator for Missouri and as a judge. He died in 1836 at the age of 51.

QUESTION

Which member of the Lewis and Clark Expedition was the first to have his account of the memorable journey published?

- A. Captain Meriwether Lewis
- B. Patrick Gass
- C. William Clark

ANSWER ON
NEXT PAGE

41

ANSWER

B

Patrick Gass had only 19 days of schooling but kept a daily journal of their trip. In 1807, the year after the Expedition's return, Gass became the first to have an account of the Expedition published. He also has the distinction of being the last survivor of the Expedition, passing away on April 30, 1870, a few weeks before his 99th birthday.

QUESTION

In what year was the northern border of the Louisiana Purchase established?

    A. 1818
    B. 1834
    C. 1865

ANSWER ON
NEXT PAGE

ANSWER

In 1818 the United States and Great Britain signed a joint occupancy agreement which set the 49th parallel as the boundary between the two countries and declared the Oregon Country to "be free and open to the vessels, citizens and subjects of both (countries)" for a period of ten years. After ten years the treaty was renewed and was officially terminated in 1846.

44

QUESTION

Who designed the keelboat, *Discovery*, used by the Lewis and Clark Expedition to transport men and supplies up the Missouri River?

    A. Thomas Jefferson
    B. Meriwether Lewis
    C. William Clark

ANSWER ON
NEXT PAGE

ANSWER

Meriwether Lewis designed the *Discovery*. She was built in Pittsburgh, Pennsylvania, and was 55 feet long, 8 feet wide and drew only 3 feet of water. She could carry 12 tons of goods and supplies and was outfitted with a square sail, 22 oars and a catwalk that allowed the crew to pole her upstream.

QUESTION

How many pounds of assorted tiny beads did the Lewis and Clark Expedition bring west with them?

- A. 33 pounds
- B. 122 pounds
- C. 237 pounds

ANSWER ON
NEXT PAGE

ANSWER

All the supplies to outfit the Lewis and Clark
Expedition were gathered at Camp Wood.
Included were goods intended for gifts
and trade with the Indian tribes they would
meet along the way. Among these items
were 33 pounds of assorted tiny beads, 500
brooches, 144 small looking glasses and
an undisclosed quantity of red and blue silk
ribbons.

QUESTION

During the Lewis and Clark Expedition what was "The Experiment" and why did it fail?

    A. Boat that sank
    B. Pack saddles that gave the horses sores
    C. Leather boots that did not hold up to the rugged conditions

ANSWER ON
NEXT PAGE

ANSWER

Meriwether Lewis designed a collapsible canoe that was dubbed *The Experiment*. It had an iron framework, consisting of 10 sections laced together with wooden ribs and animal hides. The boat sank because there was no pitch or tar to seal the seam holes and too much of the hair had been stripped off the hides causing them to leak. They were forced to leave the boat behind.

QUESTION

What is a bullboat?

    A. Another word for canoe

    B. Indian boat made from a buffalo hide

    C. Indian boat made from the bark of willow trees laid over a framework

ANSWER ON
NEXT PAGE

ANSWER

A bullboat was a floating device designed by Indians and incorporated a circular framework made of willow or cottonwood branches held together by leather strips. A buffalo hide was stretched over the framework, making a craft to transport goods and passengers. The Lewis and Clark Expedition used bullboats for transportation on the Missouri River.

QUESTION

Why did the Lewis and Clark Expedition
bring horses?

    A. For transportation
    B. To trade to the Indians
    C. For packing in food

ANSWER ON
NEXT PAGE

ANSWER

The Corps started up the Missouri with four horses ridden by hunters. When a game animal was killed, the horses were used to drag the carcass to the water's edge where it was picked up by one of the boats. Near the headwaters of the Missouri the boats were abandoned and additional horses were purchased to carry goods and supplies over the Rocky Mountains.

54

QUESTION

Camp Wood was established in 1803 at the junction of which two rivers?

- A. Kansas and Missouri rivers
- B. Yellowstone and Missouri rivers
- C. Missouri and Mississippi rivers

ANSWER ON
NEXT PAGE

ANSWER

Camp Wood, established by the Lewis and Clark Expedition in December 1803, was located in a wooded area on the east bank of the Mississippi River, directly across from the mouth of the Missouri River. It was used as a base camp and a staging area. As men were hired they were sent to the camp and put to work.

QUESTION

As the Corps navigated the lower Missouri
they had hoped to visit with the local Indians
but the Indians were gone. Where were
they?

A. Hiding from the white men
B. Hunting
C. Gathering berries in the
   mountains

ANSWER ON
NEXT PAGE

57

ANSWER

As the Corps proceeded up the Missouri
they came across many deserted Indian
villages. It was learned that the Indians were
away hunting buffalo on the Plains.

QUESTION

On July 30th, 1804 members of the Expedition met in council with the Indians along the Missouri River. What were the Indians told?

A. They would have to go to a reservation
B. They had a "Great Father"
C. They were told about the white man's God and Bibles were distributed

ANSWER ON
NEXT PAGE

59

ANSWER

B

Members of the Missouri and Oto Indian tribes, after an elaborate ceremony which featured marching, music, speeches and gifts, were told by members of the Corps that the United States now held title to the lands and the Indians were subjects of a "Great Father" who lived in the East. From that time forward the Indians would be required to obey his will.

QUESTION

Captain Lewis wrote in his journal about the technique employed by the Indian for killing buffalo. What method did he describe?

- A. Shooting buffalo with arrows
- B. Running buffalo over a cliff
- C. Roping buffalo from horseback

ANSWER ON
NEXT PAGE

61

ANSWER

B

Captain Lewis described how a warrior disguised himself with a buffalo hide and hid between a herd of buffalo and a cliff. Others stampeded the herd toward him and the buffalo runner led the herd toward the cliff, scrambled over the edge and hid in a crevice. The buffalo followed and plunged to their deaths. Often more buffalo were killed than the Indians could use.

QUESTION

The Lewis and Clark Expedition spent the winter of 1804-1805 camped near what Indian tribe?

  A. Mandan
  B. Teton Sioux
  C. Yankton Sioux

ANSWER ON
NEXT PAGE

ANSWER

The Corps spent the winter of 1804-1805 along the Missouri River near the Mandan Indian villages. They constructed Fort Mandan, a series of wooden sheds. The roofs were made of planks covered with clay, sod and grass. The Corps remained camped here until April of 1805 when they departed.

QUESTION

Name the animal that William Clark
described as being fleet of foot, with eyes
like a sheep and the body of a goat.

     A. Elk
     B. Pronghorn
     C. Deer

ANSWER ON
NEXT PAGE

ANSWER

On September 14, 1804 William Clark
killed a creature that he had never seen
before. He called it a "goat". Captain Lewis
referred to it as an "antelope". But, in fact,
the animal was neither goat nor antelope.
Having branching hollow horns that are
shed every year, the pronghorn is unique
among animals in the world.

QUESTION

Of the 106 days the Lewis and Clark Expedition spent on the Oregon coast how many days did it rain?

    A. 67 days
    B. 85 days
    C. 96 days

ANSWER ON
NEXT PAGE

67

ANSWER

C

During the Expedition's stay along the Oregon coast the rain fell 96 days and the diaries mentioned how miserable the constant rain made living conditions. On March 23, 1806, the company departed Fort Clatsop. By then their store of supplies was greatly reduced and many of the men were suffering from illnesses caused by the wet weather.

QUESTION

How many expeditions did President Thomas Jefferson send out to explore the frontiers of the North American continent?

    A. One
    B. Two
    C. Four

ANSWER ON
NEXT PAGE

69

ANSWER

Thomas Jefferson sent out four expeditions. The first was the Lewis and Clark Expedition to the Pacific coast. He also sent Zebulon Pike on an expedition to locate the source of the Mississippi and on a second expedition to explore the central Plains as far as the Rocky Mountains. The fourth group was the Freeman-Curtis Expedition that explored the Arkansas and Red Rivers.

QUESTION

How did Charles Floyd, one of the original members of the Lewis and Clark Expedition, die?

    A. Bullet wound

    B. Flu

    C. Appendicitis

ANSWER ON
NEXT PAGE

71

ANSWER

Charles Floyd joined the Corps in 1803. On August 18, 1804 Floyd became ill with stomach cramps but he attended a council with the Oto and Missouri Indians. Shortly afterward he died of what is now believed to have been appendicitis, the only member of the Lewis and Clark Expedition to die during the journey. He was buried near a creek which bears his name.

QUESTION

What was the nickname given to
Sacagawea's baby?

- A. Clark
- B. Mandan
- C. Pomp

ANSWER ON
NEXT PAGE

73

ANSWER

On February 11, 1805, while the Corps was camped at Fort Mandan, Sacagawea gave birth to a boy named Jean Baptiste, but who was called "Pomp". Pomp became a mountain man, scout, guide and miner. In 1866 he was on his way from California to a new gold strike in Montana when he was stricken with pneumonia and died. He was buried at Inskip Station in southeastern Oregon.

QUESTION

Name the hunter who was allowed to leave the Lewis and Clark Expedition before it reached St. Louis.

    A. John Ordway
    B. John Colter
    C. Alexander Willard

ANSWER ON
NEXT PAGE

ANSWER

B

John Colter was hired as a hunter for the Expedition in 1803. On the return leg, at the Mandan villages, Colter asked for and was granted his release so he could trap the upper reaches of the Missouri River. He went on to lead an adventurous life and is credited with being the first white man into the Yellowstone country. He died about 1812.

QUESTION

What type of pet did Meriwether Lewis bring on the Expedition?

- A. Cat
- B. Dog
- C. Pets were not allowed

ANSWER ON
NEXT PAGE

77

ANSWER

B

Meriwether Lewis acquired a Newfoundland dog while purchasing supplies for the expedition. He named it Seaman and the dog served as a hunter, a watchdog and as a curiosity to the Indians who thought it was a tame bear. The fate of Seaman is debated. Some say he did not finish the journey and others claim he outlived Captain Lewis.

QUESTION

How many elk were killed during the Corps'
stay at Fort Clatsop?

    A. 55
    B. 109
    C. 131

ANSWER ON
NEXT PAGE

ANSWER

During the Corps' stay at Fort Clatsop, from December 1805 through March 1806, hunters killed 131 Roosevelt elk. In addition to providing meat, the animal's hides were tanned and used for making shirts and leggings and more than 330 pairs of moccasins. The fat served as material for making candles.

80

QUESTION

Which member of the Corps kept a journal that was not published until nearly a century after his death?

- A. George Shannon
- B. Pierre Cruzatte
- C. John Ordway

ANSWER ON
NEXT PAGE

81

ANSWER

John Ordway was born in New Hampshire
and served in the military. He served the
Corps as a sergeant, kept a daily journal
and accompanied Captain Lewis and the
Mandan Chief Big White to Washington,
D.C., in 1806. Afterward he married and
became a successful farmer. He died in
1817. His journals were not published until
1916.

QUESTION

How were Cameahwait and Sacagawea related?

- A. Cousins
- B. Sisters
- C. Brother and sister

ANSWER ON
NEXT PAGE

83

ANSWER

Cameahwait was chief of the Shoshone band that occupied the Lemhi Pass along the Continental Divide. Sacagawea was a member of the Shoshone but as a young girl she had been captured by the Hidatsa, a neighboring tribe, and forced into slavery. Translating for the Expedition she suddenly recognized Cameahwait as her brother.

QUESTION

Name the deer that was described by
members of the Corps as being about
a third larger than the Eastern deer with
exceptionally large ears and a rather small
tail.

- A. White-tailed deer
- B. Mule deer
- C. Black-tailed deer

ANSWER ON
NEXT PAGE

85

ANSWER

Deer found on the Plains were unlike the deer Lewis and Clark were accustomed to in the East. These animals were bigger, with darker hair and much heavier antlers. What impressed them most were the animals' long ears. Captain Lewis named these animals mule deer.

QUESTION

The United States and what other country
negotiated the Louisiana Purchase?

    A. France
    B. Spain
    C. Russia

ANSWER ON
NEXT PAGE

87

ANSWER

President Jefferson received reports that Napoleon Bonaparte, leader of France, was hoping to establish a North American empire in the province of Louisiana. The United States opened negotiations to purchase New Orleans but Napoleon offered to sell the entire Louisiana Territory to the United States for a mere $15 million, or about 3 cents an acre.

QUESTION

How many men from the Corps did it take to bring the first buffalo into camp?

    A. One
    B. Five
    C. Twelve

ANSWER ON
NEXT PAGE

ANSWER

August 23, 1804 the first buffalo was killed by a member of the Corps. Twelve men were required to bring the carcass to camp and that night the men feasted. As the Expedition continued moving across the Plains, buffalo meat sustained the men until they reached the Rocky Mountains and passed beyond the range of the animals.

QUESTION

Who was "Big White"?

    A. Buffalo
    B. Trapper
    C. Indian

ANSWER ON
NEXT PAGE

ANSWER

Big White was chief of the lower Mandan villages where Lewis and Clark established a winter fort in 1804 and provided the Corps with food and information that proved invaluable to the Expedition. On the return leg Big White was persuaded to accompany the Expedition to Washington, D.C., and on December 31, 1806 Chief Big White met President Jefferson.

QUESTION

Who is believed to have accidentally shot
Meriwether Lewis while they were hunting
elk?

A. Charles Floyd
B. Pierre Cruzatte
C. William Clark

ANSWER ON
NEXT PAGE

ANSWER

B

Pierre Cruzatte joined the expedition in May 1804. He had lost one eye and was nearsighted in the other. This might have caused Cruzatte to accidentally mistake Captain Lewis for an elk and shoot him in the upper thigh. Lewis survived. After the Expedition Cruzatte returned to his life as a mountain man and is believed to have died in a fight with the Blackfeet in the 1820s.

QUESTION

Who could speak seven languages and was considered the best scout, hunter, and marksman of the Lewis and Clark Expedition?

    A. John Colter
    B. George Drouillard
    C. John Ordway

ANSWER ON NEXT PAGE

ANSWER

B

George Drouillard proved to be a valuable asset to the Corps as an interpreter. He was also an expert hunter and marksman. At Fort Clatsop he returned from a hunt with seven elk. After the Expedition, Drouillard went back to his mountain man life. He was killed by Blackfeet Indians in May 1910 while trapping beaver along the Jefferson River.

QUESTION

What Nez Perce chief aided the members of the Corps, taught them to make dugout canoes, and watched over their horses and saddles while they continued their journey to the Pacific Ocean?

    A. Chief Joseph
    B. Twisted Hair
    C. Chief Lolo

ANSWER ON
NEXT PAGE

ANSWER

Chief Twisted Hair met the Corps and gave the visitors dried salmon and camas flour to eat and taught them how to make dugout canoes using fire to hollow out the log. He offered to watch over the Corps' 38 horses, saddles and other equipment and proved to be a man of his word when the Lewis and Clark Expedition returned in June 1806.

QUESTION

Who was married to Sacagawea?

- A. Toussaint Charbonneau
- B. Pierre Cruzatte
- C. Jean Baptiste Charbonneau

ANSWER ON
NEXT PAGE

99

ANSWER

In about 1758 Toussaint Charbonneau was born in Canada of French and Indian descent. In the late 1790s he acquired two Shoshone captives as wives. One of these was Sacagawea. Charbonneau was thought to be about 47 years old when he signed on as an interpreter for the Corps on the journey to the Pacific Ocean and it believed he died about 1840.

QUESTION

Name the Corpsman who became known as "Peg Leg".

- A. John Potts
- B. George Shannon
- C. John Colter

ANSWER ON
NEXT PAGE

ANSWER

After meeting with President Jefferson, Chief Big White was returning home when Arikara Indians attacked the party. George Shannon, a member of the Corps, was with this group guarding Chief Big White and was severely wounded. His leg had to be amputated. After this he was known as "Peg Leg" Shannon.

QUESTION

Who served as a blacksmith and was
punished for misconduct while a member of
the Lewis and Clark Expedition?

- A. Alexander Willard
- B. John Colter
- C. Charles Floyd

ANSWER ON
NEXT PAGE

103

ANSWER

Alexander Willard served as the blacksmith for the Lewis and Clark Expedition. On July 11, 1804 he was found asleep on sentry duty, a serious offense that could have endangered the lives of the Corpsmen. Willard was punished with 100 lashes. The remainder of the journey he served with distinction.

QUESTION

How many Indians were killed by members of the Lewis and Clark Expedition?

  A. None
  B. Two
  C. Thirty-four

ANSWER ON
NEXT PAGE

ANSWER

B

During the return, four members of the Lewis and Clark Expedition, including Meriwether Lewis, were involved in a fight with a band of Blackfeet Indians over the theft of several of the Corps' rifles and horses. Two Indians were killed in the short battle. Lewis's party was able to escape.

QUESTION

What was the greatest pest the members of the Lewis and Clark Expedition were forced to endure?

- A. Rats
- B. Mosquitoes
- C. Cockroaches

ANSWER ON NEXT PAGE

107

ANSWER

B

Mosquitoes were very troublesome to the members of the Lewis and Clark Expedition. Bites became infected. Bugs flew into mouths, noses, eyes and ears. On July 15, 1806 Captain Lewis wrote in his journal that the mosquitoes "continue to infest us in a manner that we can scarcely exist.... My dog even howls with the torture...."

QUESTION

How high were the Great Falls of the Missouri?

    A. 31 feet
    B. 124 feet
    C. 360 feet

ANSWER ON NEXT PAGE

ANSWER

The Lewis and Clark Expedition reached the Great Falls of the Missouri River in July, 1805. Here they found the river dropped in a series of five major falls. The total elevation difference was 360 feet and it required 17 days of hard work to portage the goods and supplies around the falls.

QUESTION

What mountain range did the Corps cross on the Nez Perce Trail?

- A. Bitterroot Mountains
- B. Rocky Mountains
- C. Cascade Mountains

ANSWER ON
NEXT PAGE

ANSWER

The Nez Perce Trail led over the Bitterroot Mountains and, even though the Corps crossed at Lolo Pass, they found the trail was steep and rocky. They encountered downed windfall trees, snow drifts, sparse grass for the horses and hardly any wild game. The crossing took eleven days. To keep from starving, the men were forced to kill and eat three of their horses.

QUESTION

The Indians believed that killing a grizzly bear was comparable to killing what?

    A. White buffalo
    B. An enemy
    C. Bull elk

ANSWER ON
NEXT PAGE

113

ANSWER

Grizzly bears were unknown to the members of the Lewis and Clark Expedition until they killed a grizzly on April 29, 1804. They gave the claws, as a gift, to an Indian chief who considered killing a grizzly comparable to taking the life of a mortal enemy on the field of battle.

QUESTION

How many members of the Lewis and Clark Expedition kept daily diaries of the journey?

- A. Two
- B. Four
- C. Seven

ANSWER ON
NEXT PAGE

115

ANSWER

President Jefferson required that both
Lewis and Clark keep a daily record of
their travels. The co-captains urged others
to record their observations. In April 1805
Captain Lewis wrote to President Jefferson
that a total of seven men were keeping
journals. Five of those journals have been
recovered but two are unaccounted for and
have never been found.

116

QUESTION

On August 12th, 1805 Captain Lewis and several others rejoiced at having reached the headwaters of what major river?

- A. Missouri
- B. Columbia
- C. Mississippi

ANSWER ON
NEXT PAGE

117

ANSWER

Upon reaching the headwaters of the Missouri River Captain Lewis noted in his diary that one of his men "exultingly stood with a foot on each side of this little rivulet and thanked his god that he had lived to bestride the mighty & heretofore deemed endless Missouri."

QUESTION

Why did members of the Lewis and Clark Expedition journey to Ecola Creek on the north end of Cannon Beach?

- A. To obtain salt
- B. Fish for salmon
- C. View a whale

ANSWER ON
NEXT PAGE

119

ANSWER

On January 5, 1806 William Clark led a group over Tillamook Head to Ecola Creek where they viewed a whale that had washed up on shore. By the time they arrived the local Indians had already stripped the blubber from the carcass and all that remained was the skeleton.

120

QUESTION

Which member of the Corps of Discovery did the Indians call Red-Headed Chief?

- A. George Shannon
- B. Pierre Cruzatte
- C. William Clark

ANSWER ON
NEXT PAGE

121

ANSWER

William Clark fought against the Cherokee
and Creek and gained a reputation for his
honesty and fairness in his dealings with
the Indians. As the Expedition traveled west
Indians along the way began calling Clark
by the name, Red-Headed Chief.

QUESTION

By what mode of transportation did President Thomas Jefferson believe the Lewis and Clark Expedition could make its way across the North American continent?

    A. Horseback
    B. By foot
    C. Boats and canoes

ANSWER ON
NEXT PAGE

ANSWER

President Jefferson believed, as did most others of his time, that a Northwest Passage linked the Atlantic and Pacific oceans and that the major waterways, the Mississippi, Missouri and Columbia rivers, would provide a nearly continuous route across the continent. It was thought that the Corps could travel, with minimal portaging, by boat and canoe.

QUESTION

How many years after the end of the Revolutionary War was the Lewis and Clark Expedition sent to explore the West?

 A. Ten years
 B. Twenty years
 C. Forty years

ANSWER ON NEXT PAGE

125

ANSWER

The Revolutionary War officially ended with the signing of the Treaty of Paris in 1783. Twenty years later the Lewis and Clark Expedition began forming at Camp Wood along the Mississippi River across from the mouth of the Missouri River.

QUESTION

What was the cost of the Louisiana Purchase?

    A. $1 million
    B. $2 million
    C. $15 million

ANSWER ON
NEXT PAGE

ANSWER

The United States government paid $15,000,000 to France for roughly 828,000 square miles of land that stretched from the Mississippi River west to the Rocky Mountains, and from Canada south to the Gulf of Mexico.

128

QUESTION

What was the Indian name given to
Sacagawea?

    A. Bird Woman
    B. Wise One
    C. One Feather

ANSWER ON
NEXT PAGE

ANSWER

The name "Bird Woman" was given to Sacagawea by the Hidatsa tribe, which stole her as a young child from her homeland along the Salmon River. She was sold to Toussaint Charbonneau and became his wife. Some historians believe she died in 1812 while others claim she was married twice, had six children and lived to be nearly 100 years old.

QUESTION

Why did Pacific coast Indians not possess horses?

    A. They had not learned to ride
    B. Horses were too expensive
    C. Horses were impractical

ANSWER ON
NEXT PAGE

131

ANSWER

Indians living along the Pacific coast moved about easily paddling canoes through an intricate system of rivers, streams and estuaries. Horses, their use limited because of the boggy marshes and the dense underbrush, were an impractical form of transportation. Also, grass was scarce in the heavily timbered forests.

QUESTION

Who named Beacon Rock on the Columbia River?

- A. Captain Cook
- B. Captain Vancouver
- C. Lewis and Clark

ANSWER ON
NEXT PAGE

133

ANSWER

The Lewis and Clark Expedition, traveling down the Columbia River, reached Beacon Rock, which they named, on November 2, 1805. They noted that this spot marked the beginning of tidewater influence from the Pacific Ocean.

QUESTION

Name the first military establishment built in Oregon.

    A.   Fort Dallas
    B.   Fort Astoria
    C.   Fort Clatsop

ANSWER ON
NEXT PAGE

135

ANSWER

Members of the Lewis and Clark Expedition built Fort Clatsop, the first military establishment in Oregon. The fort consisted of seven cabins surrounded by a fifty-foot square wooden stockade. It was occupied from December 7, 1805 until March 23, 1806.

QUESTION

About how many Indians camped at Celilo Falls when the fish were running?

    A. 500
    B. 3,000
    C. 10,000

ANSWER ON
NEXT PAGE

137

ANSWER

The Lewis and Clark Expedition passed Celilo Falls on the Columbia River between salmon runs and saw few Indians in the vicinity. But it has been estimated that 3,000 Indians from many Northwest tribes would gather to camp and fish at Celilo when the salmon were running.

QUESTION

What was the mission of the Lewis and Clark Expedition?

- A. Locate sites for fur trading posts
- B. Explore and map
- C. Search the route for the Oregon Trail

ANSWER ON
NEXT PAGE

139

ANSWER

The purpose of the Lewis and Clark Expedition was to explore and map the Missouri River and all the land between the Rocky mountains and the Pacific coast. President Thomas Jefferson also ordered an accurate journal be kept and that the soil, minerals and plants of the regions visited be cataloged and samples taken.

QUESTION

Name the one-eyed chief of the Chinook
Indians who greeted Lewis and Clark at the
mouth of the Columbia River.

    A. Concomly
    B. Sitting Bull
    C. Chief Joseph

ANSWER ON
NEXT PAGE

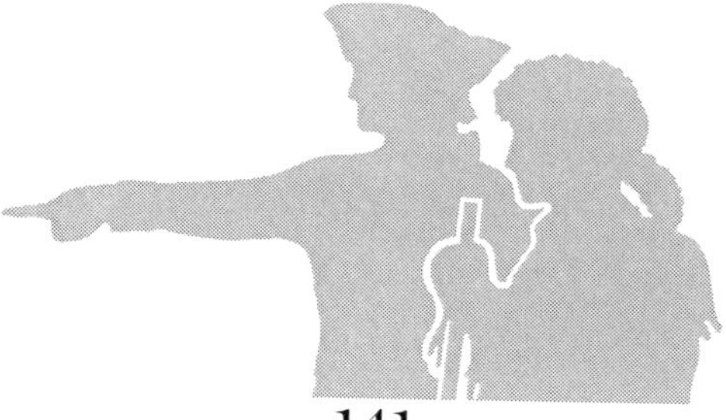

ANSWER

Lewis and Clark met Concomly, chief of the Chinook tribe, on November 20th, 1805. He was given peace medals and a small flag. In return Concomly aided the members of Corps and remained friendly as other white trappers and traders arrived. He died in 1830 as a result of an epidemic brought by the foreign visitors.

142

QUESTION

About how far does the water drop over Multnomah Falls?

    A. 511 feet
    B. 620 feet
    C. 713 feet

ANSWER ON
NEXT PAGE

ANSWER

B

Lewis and Clark made mention in their journals of a high falls on the south side of the Columbia River between the mouth of the Sandy River and the Cascades. It is not known who named Multnomah Falls but the name apparently goes back to the 1860s. The water of Multnomah Falls, in a two-tiered drop, cascades a spectacular 620 feet.

144

QUESTION

Name the food that Captain Lewis and others felt was far superior to elk or venison.

- A. Horse
- B. Beaver
- C. Dog

ANSWER ON
NEXT PAGE

145

ANSWER

C

Captain Lewis noted in his journal that the Corps had been obliged to subsist on dog meat for so long that he had grown particularly fond of it. On January 3, 1806 he wrote, "for my own part I have become so perfectly reconciled to dog that I think it an agreeable food and would prefer it vastly to lean Venison or Elk."

QUESTION

On their return, what did the Lewis and Clark Expedition trade for horses from the Indians near Hood River?

   A. Beads
   B. Kettles
   C. Cloth

ANSWER ON NEXT PAGE

147

ANSWER

When it came to trading for horses the explorers were faced with a difficult problem. They had few goods to trade. However, after lengthy negotiations, the local Indians agreed to take three kettles in exchange for five horses.

QUESTION

On the return leg, what forced the Lewis and Clark Expedition to turn back from crossing the Bitterroot Mountains?

    A. Trouble with the Indians
    B. Snow drifts
    C. Storm

ANSWER ON
NEXT PAGE

149

ANSWER

Against the advice of the Nez Perce who told them the trail over the mountains was not yet passable, the explorers, eager to return to St. Louis, started over the Bitterroots. They were forced to turn back by fifteen-foot snowdrifts. They waited several weeks before beginning a second try on June 24, 1806. They made the crossing in six days.

QUESTION

Who provided medical attention to the members of the Corps?

- A. Meriwether Lewis
- B. William Clark
- C. Sacagawea

ANSWER ON
NEXT PAGE

151

ANSWER

Lewis and Clark both provided medical assistance to the Indians, but Lewis generally acted as the Corps' principle doctor. He was called on to treat a variety of ailments including exhaustion, frostbite, malaria, diarrhea, boils, puncture wounds, typhoid fever, twisted ankles, colic and snakebites.

152

QUESTION

One of the members of the Expedition stood court-martial. What was his punishment?

- A. Firing squad
- B. Flogging
- C. Prison

ANSWER ON
NEXT PAGE

ANSWER

B

Private M.B. Reed walked away from camp and was captured on August 18, 1804. He was court-martialed and found guilty of desertion. His punishment was to run the gauntlet four times while the men of the company flogged his bare back with whips. After this he was dishonorably discharged.

QUESTION

What medicine did Captain Lewis administer to Sacagawea to relieve the pain of a difficult labor?

    A. Morphine
    B. Tea
    C. Buttons from the rattle of a
       rattlesnake

ANSWER ON
NEXT PAGE

155

ANSWER

C

Sacagawea went into labor on February 11, 1805. It was a difficult labor with a great deal of pain. Captain Lewis, using an Indian remedy, broke two buttons off the rattles of a rattlesnake, crushed them into a powder, added water and had Sacagawea drink the concoction. Ten minutes later she gave birth to a healthy boy.

QUESTION

How did the Clatsop Indians cook their food?

- A. Roasted over a campfire
- B. Cooked in iron kettles
- C. Boiled in wooden bowls with hot stones

ANSWER ON
NEXT PAGE

ANSWER

The Clatsop Indians carved their bowls from a solid piece of wood. On January 17, 1806 Captain Lewis explained how the local Indians cooked, writing in his journal, "in these vessels they boil their fish or flesh by means of hot stones which they immerce in the water with the article to be boiled."

QUESTION

How much did Meriwether Lewis estimate it would cost to outfit an overland expedition to the Pacific Ocean?

- A. $2,500
- B. $20,000
- C. $100,000

ANSWER ON
NEXT PAGE

ANSWER

Lewis told President Jefferson he thought he could lead an expedition to the Pacific coast and back for an expenditure of $2,500. The actual investment turned out to be much higher, considered to be almost $40,000.

QUESTION

How many miles a day did the returning Corps travel on the lower Missouri River?

    A. 20 miles
    B. 40 miles
    C. 80 miles

ANSWER ON
NEXT PAGE

ANSWER

The men were traveling fast, paddling with the current down the Missouri and making as many as 80 miles a day.

QUESTION

What did the American public think had happened to the Lewis and Clark Expedition during the more than two years they spent in the wilderness?

A. Lost
B. Killed by Indians
C. Held prisoner by the Russians

ANSWER ON NEXT PAGE

163

ANSWER

B

Many rumors were circulated regarding the fate of the Expedition. These rumors included massacred by Indians, eaten by wild animals, and imprisoned by Spanish soldiers. When the Corps swept into St. Louis at noon on September 23, 1806, there was much rejoicing upon their safe return.

QUESTION

How many months did the Lewis and Clark Expedition spend in the wilderness?

- A. 14 months
- B. 19 months
- C. 28 months

ANSWER ON NEXT PAGE

ANSWER

The Lewis and Clark Expedition departed from Camp Wood on May 14, 1804 and returned on September 23, 1806. The entire trip to the Pacific Ocean and back had taken a total of 28 months and 10 days.

QUESTION

Name the domesticated animal that members of the Corps spotted as they neared St. Louis and was cause for great rejoicing.

- A. Sheep
- B. Cow
- C. Goat

ANSWER ON NEXT PAGE

167

ANSWER

B

On September 20, 1806 the Expedition reached the settlement of LaCharette and the men saw the first milk cow they had seen in more than two years. The men fired their rifles in a show of appreciation and that evening they celebrated long into the night.

168

QUESTION

How many miles did the Lewis and Clark Expedition travel through the wilderness of North America?

- A. 3,000 miles
- B. 5,000 miles
- C. More than 7,000 miles

ANSWER ON NEXT PAGE

169

ANSWER

The total number of miles traveled varied according to each man due to the many scouting trips and side trips for the purpose of exploring or hunting. But without a doubt all members of the party traveled at least 7,000 miles on the Expedition.

QUESTION

As the members of the Lewis and Clark Expedition neared St. Louis, crowds gathered along the riverbank. How did the public salute the Corps' achievement?

    A. Set free balloons
    B. Fired rifles
    C. Threw rose petals

ANSWER ON
NEXT PAGE

171

ANSWER

As the Corps swept downriver, cheering crowds gathered along the banks and fired gunpowder salutes as a sign of respect for what the members of the Expedition had been able to accomplish.

QUESTION

How much were Charbonneau and Sacagawea paid for their involvement with the Lewis and Clark Expedition?

A. $500
B. $1,000
C. $2,500

ANSWER ON
NEXT PAGE

ANSWER

Charbonneau and Sacagawea returned to the Mandan villages along with the baby, Pomp, who was by now 19 months old. They received a payment of $500 for their time and involvement with the Expedition.

QUESTION

Christmas 1805 was celebrated at Fort Clatsop. The men who smoked were presented with tobacco. What did the non-smokers receive as a gift from Lewis and Clark?

- A. Nothing
- B. Whiskey
- C. Handkerchief

ANSWER ON NEXT PAGE

175

ANSWER

The men who did not smoke were each
given a handkerchief as a present. But the
celebration was short-lived. William Clark
wrote in his journal that all they had to eat
that day was spoiled elk meat, pounded
fishmeal that had turned rancid and a few
bowls of roots.

QUESTION

Which member of the Lewis and Clark Expedition carved his name into the rock of Pompy's Pillar?

- A. Lewis
- B. Clark
- C. Charbonneau

ANSWER ON NEXT PAGE

ANSWER

Traveling along the Yellowstone River, William Clark stopped at a prominent rock which he named Pompy's Tower in honor of Sacagawea's child. He carved "W. Clark" and the date "July 25, 1806" into the rock. The name of the landmark was changed to Pompy's Pillar but Clark's signature is still visible, protected from weather and vandals by a thick layer of glass.

178

QUESTION

When Chief Big White returned to the
Mandan village after visiting Washington,
D.C., and the President of the United States,
how was he received by his people?

    A. As a hero
    B. With contempt and ridicule
    C. Regaled as a brave warrior

ANSWER ON
NEXT PAGE

179

ANSWER

After three years away, Chief Big White told his people about meeting President Jefferson, his White House reception where he had been treated as a celebrity, and his tours of fascinating Eastern cities. Big White was shocked when his people called him a liar; later, when he wore his military uniform, they mocked him.

QUESTION

How many new animal species and subspecies did Lewis and Clark find on their journey to the Pacific Ocean?

    A. 27
    B. 84
    C. 122

ANSWER ON
NEXT PAGE

181

ANSWER

The Lewis and Clark Expedition was credited with discovering and describing 122 animal species and subspecies that were not known to science at that time. These included the prairie dog, porcupine, jackrabbit, grizzly bear and coyote as well as terns, jays, trumpeter swans, mountain quail, woodpeckers, steelhead and salmon.

QUESTION

Members of the Corps killed two Blackfeet Indians. What was done with the bodies of the fallen warriors?

- A. Buried
- B. Burned
- C. Left as they lay

ANSWER ON
NEXT PAGE

183

ANSWER

Captain Lewis directed the bodies of the Blackfeet be left as they lay. Their shields, bows and arrows were gathered and burned and Captain Lewis placed a peace medal around the neck of one of the dead men. Fearing revenge, the explorers rode their horses hard and fast and managed to cover a distance of 120 miles over the next 24 hours.

184

QUESTION

The Chinook and Clatsop Indians inhabited which present-day state?

    A. Oregon
    B. Idaho
    C. Montana

ANSWER ON
NEXT PAGE

185

ANSWER

The Chinook and Clatsop Indians lived along the lower reaches of the Columbia River. This area is now part of the state of Oregon.

QUESTION

Descendants of the Nez Perce Indians who befriended members of the Lewis and Clark Expedition inhabited which present-day state?

    A. Idaho
    B. Oregon
    C. North Dakota

ANSWER ON
NEXT PAGE

187

ANSWER

The descendants of the Nez Perce Indians, who came to the aid of the Lewis and Clark Expedition after their struggles to cross the Bitterroot Mountains, live in the present day state of Idaho.

QUESTION

In which two present-day states can be found members of the Hidatsa, Mandan, Arikara and Teton Sioux Indian tribes?

- A. Oregon and Washington
- B. Idaho and Montana
- C. North and South Dakota

ANSWER ON
NEXT PAGE

189

ANSWER

C

As the Lewis and Clark Expedition passed along the Missouri River through the present-day states of North and South Dakota, they passed through territory dominated by the Hidatsa, Mandan, Arikara and Teton Sioux Indian tribes.

QUESTION

Traveling down the Columbia River, how did members of the Corps know they were getting close to the ocean?

- A. By the way the Indians were dressed
- B. Seagulls
- C. Seals

ANSWER ON NEXT PAGE

191

ANSWER

As the explorers reached the falls at The Dalles they spotted an Indian wearing a sailor's jacket. They knew that the jacket came from a British or Yankee ship and had most likely been traded for furs. This led to the belief that the Expedition must be close to the coast.

Wild West Trivia series was written and designed by award-winning author, Rick Steber. He has written more than forty books and has sold more than a million copies. For a complete listing of his books, or to see other titles in the Wild West Trivia series, visit www.ricksteber.com